AF482888

Theory and Practice of *La Verdadera Destreza*

Theory and Practice of *La Verdadera Destreza*

ALBERTO BOMPREZZI

ACKNOWLEDGMENTS

This book would have not been possible without the invaluable help of many people: first of all to all my students and that allows me to make my living doing what I love most, Fencing and teaching Fencing. Among them I must particularly thank those who help me running the school daily, helping me with the classes, organizing activities and taking care of the salle when I am forced to travel or being absent from the school:

Maestro Marc Gener
Maestro Óscar Torres
Instructor Juan Manuel Muñoz
Instructor Francisco Puerta
Instructor José Salazar

And, at last but not least, Maestro Carlos Urgel who has worked with me closely to help me publish this first book. Without any of them I could not have done it.

And finally I would like to thank all those who have helped me through the years, in a way or another they are also a part of this.

INTRODUCTION

This book has humble objectives: I only aspire to help those who have an interest in *La Verdadera Destreza* understand how it works and how it can be used.

Once it is understood, *Destreza* is pretty simple, the complex part being its practical implementation, something which is usually not explained in books. In the following pages, I try to contextualise some tools so they can be used freely by anyone who wishes to study *Destreza*, no matter their approach. Understanding what these tools are and the different ways they may be applied can be useful for those interested in the reconstruction of the old methods but also for those who aim for a more practical and effective approach; Because they are theoretical tools, the physical implementation may vary but stay respectful to the principles established by *La Verdadera Destreza*

The practical execution may change substantially depending on the context; those fencers interested in the old methods would try to stay closer to the descriptions offered by the treatises while those with an interest in a more effective and modern approach shall focus on the body mechanics as a way to develop modern and effective *Destreza* practice styles.

The reality is that I work and teach in both fields; in this book, the practical approach shown is the modern Art, which has been developed for the modern-day context with masks, protective gear, rubber blunts, and sneakers; but the theoretical tools may be used to teach the old methods too, which, in my opinion, must be reconstructed respecting the context of its age, which means assuming we are not going to wear any masks and almost no protective gear and that gentlemen like us do not want to lose an eye and at the same time need to avoid harming our adversaries.

It is obvious that we do not fence as they did, not because we do not want to but because we can't. What we do may be similar in some cases, while in others it will be not, but this should not be a problem. *La Verdadera Destreza*, the Art of Fencing, is an Art and the important thing is fencing correctly, in an organized manner, with strength and control, in a mechanically efficient, strong and technically correct way. It doesn't matter which context we have chosen; we should always fence correctly if we want *Destreza* to be respected, used and admired.

Why I never focus exclusively in the reconstruction of the old methods is easy to explain: I know that nowadays, in any martial art, respect is gained by how well we fence, by hitting often and properly and by not be hit ourselves, and the old methods were not designed for this modern approach; as a consequence, they do not work in modern day free sparring. Having to start somewhere, I decided a long time ago to develop a modern day *Destreza* practical method that would allow the modern day *diestro* to face fencers from other schools effectively, rather than simply trying to reconstruct the old methods as they were, because, as we know, they do not work for our times. Besides, I felt that I was doing just the same thing the old masters did: Pacheco never thought about reconstructing Carranza, and Ettenhard and Lorenz de Rada never tried to do things as Pacheco described them; on the contrary, both made the method evolve, developing a new practical style, and somewhat changing the Theory, which was necessary to explain what they were doing. Both Ettenhard and Rada did this, and that is also what I have done throughout the years when I felt it was necessary. I am sure that some people may argue that it is arrogant on my side to change the old theory, but on the contrary: it is plain and simple intellectual honesty.

Modern day context is very different from the context in which Rada lived, which was different from the context in which Ettenhard lived, and different from the context in which Pacheco lived; being this the case, why should I stick to descriptions that clearly do not work nowadays, when in the old days the old masters themselves made changes to the original method designed by Pacheco de Narváez? How can we pretend not to make changes after 400 years when they made changes less than 40 years later?

Changes are necessary if we want to fence properly, they really are if we want *Destreza* to be True. And, for me at least, the important thing is to fence correctly, because in the end Fencing is just Fencing, is the Art of the Sword is, no matter the school, or the age in which a treatise was written. Treatises are a tool to develop good, solid and efficient modern-day methods in order to create a new tradition of good, well trained, and educated fencers.

Destreza is our method but we do not have to keep doing things as they were done in the past if they no longer work; if we kept doing them despise this, it would be bad and it would go against the most basic *Destreza* principle, because if it does not work it is not true, it is not universal, and it cannot be considered a part of science. We must change things so that they remain true in the current day.

The Truth of the old days is not true nowadays; we must identify this –which can only be done sword in hand, fencing, training and sparring– and from there develop new practical methods. Some will be better, some will be worse, and like in the old days, those better structured and organized will lead the way. We need new methods that must be tested in the field and when practical differences appear with the old manners, we must make the necessary changes in the Theory to offer not only our students, but also to those who will follow, a coherent and well explained method of *La Verdadera Destreza*.

This does not mean that reconstructing must be left aside, it is important and attractive. But in my opinion, when we talk about Theory intellectual honesty must come first, and the study and reconstruction of the old methods second; doing it the other way is like pretending to play ancient music with ancient instruments without knowing how to play modern music with modern instruments.

In saying this I am not targeting anyone. I know how difficult it is to practice historical fencing nowadays and *La Verdadera Destreza* even more; my aim is to explain my approach, which in the end it is just doing the same thing the old masters did in their time: to adapt the old method to our modern day context so we can teach and help modern day *diestros* to become good fencers that will bring respect and admiration to the method we follow and love.

I sincerely believe that in doing so we will better serve the memory of the old masters than by simply trying to do what they did. These are new times, and therefore new methods and new masters are needed to create a new tradition that comes from the old one but that can't be exactly the way it was.

But even for those not interested in a more effective and practical approach I hope that this book can help them look at the *Destreza* from another perspective.

Please forgive me if I was not able to explain well enough but this can't be denied: I know how to implement the Theory correctly in all possible fields.

Maestro Mayor Alberto Bomprezzi
Asociación Española de Esgrima Antigua
Escuela de Esgrima Histórica de Madrid

1. BASICS

This short text on *Destreza* lists a number of questions I have received and explanations I have had to give to a good number of students in my school when they were preparing for their grade exams; and given that there are few resources available in English I have decided to write some brief explanations hoping they can be of some help to all those who are interested in *La Verdadera Destreza.*

The text is not meant to be exhaustive in any way. A second text with additional information will be published in the future. There are many details that are not explained, but I hope that at least the way I approach the study of *Destreza,* adapting it to the context in which I live to make it understandable and useful for the modern day fencer, is understood.

The approach I have always followed is simple:

- Practice comes first. Training is more important than reading treatises. The latter will be very important eventually, but this will happen further down the road. Learn train footwork, thrusts, cuts, weapon handling, before trying to do what the treatise says. Otherwise it would like trying to play an ancient instrument not even knowing how to play a modern one.
- Fencing well is paramount. The most important thing is: be a good *Destreza* fencer, don't fence as we think they did back in the day. The reconstruction of what they did may be a fun activity but it is not the most important one. I use *Destreza* to learn and teach people to be good fencers, I don't try to fence exactly as I imagine they did in the 17th century. I do it from time to time, for fun, that's all. *Destreza* is a tool, not an end in itself.

- If the way we fence works only when our opponent fences the same way we do, then we are not fencing correctly. A good fencer must be able to adapt. We fence with masks and sneakers and we can't change that. That means that we can move faster and assume risks we would not assume without them. Pretending we are not wearing protection is unrealistic and it eventually leads to bad fencing. We are modern day fencers, there is no point in denying it.

If the practical method is not effective, *Destreza* will not get any credit. It does not matter if we are being faithful to the treatises or not, that's irrelevant. If we fence poorly, with lack of order, poor body mechanics and bad weapon handling, we will be not helping *Destreza* in any way. If we say that what we do is historical, but we do not fence properly, the word "historical" is immediately considered as an excuse to justify poor fencing. *La Verdadera Destreza* deserves, in my opinion, to be better considered and to achieve this good practical method developed.

Some years ago, a good *Destreza* student was fencing against an Italian friend who is a skilled fencer and while trying to make *atajo*, he received a good number of hits and was unable to put it in practice properly, as his adversary was disengaging quickly every time. When the assault was over, he came to me and told me *"El atajo no funciona"* (The *atajo* does not work) and I explained to him that the problem was not the atajo but the way he was implementing it. To show him, I fenced with our Italian friend, hit him many times while being rarely hit though I was unable to get a single strong *atajo*. Then I went back to my student and told him more or less this: *"The atajo is a mean, a tool, not an obligation. You use it if you can, if it is useful, if it is not you do not do it. The aim, the real aim is controlling the central line, which can be achieved in many ways, through the right angle –the arm extended, so all type of thrusts and counterguards–, with slight subtle binds, with strong binds, and normally through combinations of all things together, as the adversary will never cooperate and will try to stop you. Very often we only make counterguards –atajo virtual– but we are unable to bind strong, and this is not a problem as long as we control the central line."*

It's funny how often we like to fit things into categories, and this is exactly what was happening with my student in this particular case. He created an image in his mind of what he should do to use *Destreza*, using the right angle to approach the opponent, the *atajo* and then the thrust, the cut, or the disarm, the three universal means, one after the other. Simple, but completely unrealistic.

The problem is that, by reading treatises, he was creating a mental image of how *Destreza* should be and tried to use. But the image created was wrong and for that reason did not work well. He tried to implement what he thought *Destreza* says, not what *Destreza* really says.

Why would he do this? Not on purpose, obviously, but the image we create comes from our experience, our set of values, and basically the world in which we live, which is very different from that of the old *Destreza* authors. Or to put it more clearly, it is very possible that many times we do not understand what the authors really meant, we think we do but we do not.

But how can we learn what *Destreza* really says, while avoiding to create an image that can blind us?

First of all, I would suggest starting from the beginning; I mean training, fencing, thinking of what is happening and trying to understand without preconceiving any technique. And then, learn the theory, the pure theory.

Destreza is, for what matters now, a theory. Just a theory,

not a practice. As a theory, it is divided in two parts:
1. The pure theory.
2. The practical theory.

There is a third part, the practice, also called the Art. But it is not part of the theory.

THE PURE THEORY

The Pure Theory is all the terms and concepts created to define space, so parameters can be established, and distances and angles measured. This part also includes the tools to analyze distance, angles and timing. The Means –*Los Medios*–, which is, in my experience, the most important part of all the *Destreza* theory. It is a powerful tool because, instead of being built on time, a concept that can't be measured objectively but only perceived in the Art, the Spanish method is built on tridimensional distance. This is why at the beginning it may appear more complex, because all other methods are based on time. It is also the reason why most people misunderstand *Destreza* when they study it: they still have a time mindset, so they focus more on the universal means as techniques rather than as general concepts.

Though most fencers think of this as secondary and pay little attention to it, in fact it is not. It is the most important part, because by being theoretical it is timeless and universal. It is what allows us to measure the different parts of a fencing action.

The pure theory is in a certain way simply descriptive geometry, but instead of being applied to architecture or design, it is applied to fencing, and it can be used to study time and distance in all weapons. But there is something important to remember: the use of the pure theory depends on the practical skills of the fencer with the weapon; the more skilled and experienced, the more they will take from it.

Theory cannot transform a beginner into an expert, or an average fencer into a legendary *diestro*; It is up to each of us to become as good as we can. But it can help us become better fencers and teachers.

The pure theory may be applied to all kind of weapons as it is nothing more than a body of terms and concepts created to explain and measure movement in the fencing assault. It can be easily combined with methods from other traditions like the Italian, French, or German; in fact, with all of them. One friend of mine has adapted *Destreza* parts into his Wing Chun teaching method.

In the Italian method the pure theory is very small, only including the parts related to the study of time and distance, but no tools are given for it, all is left in the hands of the practical skills of the fencer. *Un tempo, due tempi, contra-tempo, mezzo tempo, misura lunga, misura stretta* are some of the terms and concepts that correspond to the Italian pure theory.

THE PRACTICAL THEORY

The Practical Theory are *Los Medios Universales*, the Right Angle, the bind and the disarm. *Ángulo recto, atajo* and *movimiento de conclusión, las reglas generales* and *tretas particulares*, all of them must be understood under the light of the pure theory, the Means, and the control of the central line, if we do not want to make wrong assumptions.

The practical theory explains how the basic fencing actions should be performed but leaving the details in the implementation to the skill and experience of the fencer, obviously. A book is not the best tool to teach something practical, there is no way to learn how to throw a football as Tom Brady by reading books on football; practice and skill are necessary to do this.

All the Practical theory, in general, does not describe techniques, but establishes general concepts that go over a large amount of positions and techniques that share something in common. There are exceptions, as Pacheco's first book spends a lot of pages describing techniques and other treatises such as Tamariz's also describe some, but in general *Destreza* authors do not focus on techniques.

The Practical theory does not work well on two handed weapons, though it works well in all kind of one-handed weapons. In the Italian method, 90% of the treatises are Practical Theory, –guards and techniques are in fact the Italian Practical Theory–, this is why the possibility of using it for the study of other type of weapons is limited.

THE PRACTICE OF THE ART

This leads to the third part of *Destreza*, the Practice, which we also call the Art. This is what we do in the salle, practicing thrusts, binding, disengaging or disarming, sparring. The Art is achieved through training and depends strongly on individual skills. Physical prowess, stamina, concentration, neuromuscular coordination, speed, are a natural gift that, if properly trained, will deliver great fencers.

The Art is what great fencers offer to Fencing and what teachers offer to their students, their practical knowledge achieved through years of training and studying, that can help others learn to fence correctly.

The Art cannot be learned from a book as it is something physical; the only way to learn it is by training. It is the Art, the Practice, that gives birth to the Theory. It has always been like that; first comes the practical activity, fencing with swords, then the will and the need to understand, and consequently, theoretical methods appear. Some will be more abstract, some more practical, but they all have the same purpose; to transmit knowledge, to explain fencing and to help fence properly.

But the Art lies first, always, in Fencing and in all other activities that have a practical side.

MUSIC AND DESTREZA

An example that I often use when people ask me about Theory and Practice in *Destreza* comes from Music, an Art which is much better known than ours. We can't forget that, in Spanish language, the term we use to describe footwork is compass, a term that has a clear musical meaning.

The Pure Theory is the sol-fa, the music sheet with notes, compasses, beats… all elements that helps us read the music sheet and read, transmit and play music. Instead of the music sheet we use the circle, the diameter, the angles, the movements, the Means.

The Practical Theory are the general rules to properly play the instrument, the body and finger positions, the chords, the harmonies, the rhythm, the melodies.

The Practice or the Art is the action of playing music with the instrument, to create sounds. The music that we make may be beautiful or awful: that depends on how well we play the instrument, a guitar, a piano, or, in our case, a sword.

It is possible to be an extraordinary musician without knowing sol-fa, as a consequence of an extraordinary talent, but in general, good musicians study the musical technique so they can write it, transmit it, and play with others. Sol-fa is the language of music, *Destreza* is a language for fencing. The language is the same for all instruments, though it doesn't help play them: one can be great with the guitar and not as good with the saxo, or the piano, just as in fencing when we change swords.

In Music, knowing the language does not make you a great musician or composer, and it is the same in fencing. Knowing *Destreza* terms and theory does not make a *diestro*. This depends on how well he plays the instrument, in our case, the sword.

Sol-fa is normally studied and learned singing, as a complement for practical lessons with the instrument. At the beginning, during the first years, one may feel it is useless, as they cannot find the relationship between the notes, the chords, the scales, and the rhythms, the harmonies and the melodies, but in time they will become clear. But this is achieved through constant practice with the instrument, to achieve technical competence with it; without it, sol-fa is useless. It is a mean, a tool to create, transmit and play Music not an end in itself.

The same thing happens with *Destreza*; the definition of space, the Means, the use of the angles, may seem too abstract and useless at the beginning, as everything happens so fast in the assault that many details are difficult to perceive; but in time, when mechanics are interiorized, the theory becomes really useful. As in Music, we realize that there is an order in Fencing, but to perceive it we need training; it doesn't matter how much we read: we cannot understand what we are reading if we do not have practical experience. And it is a tool, something we use to fence properly, which is the real goal.

But the most important thing is that, like Sol-fa, *Destreza's* Pure Theory is timeless and universal, completely independent from the social, technological and historical context; so while the Universal Means may be different because of the context, the Pure Theory is not; even more, it can help us find out how the Universal Means must be performed nowadays to stay true.

2. LINES, CIRCLES AND PLANES

Destreza treatises normally spend some time explaining the basic elements of pure theory. I will do it too, but in a short, very basic way, with the simple intention of creating a sort of fencing sheet, just like a music sheet that anyone can use to study fencing.

Please consider that all the geometrical figures described can be used freely by the *diestro* or teacher to explain and analyze the phrase of arms, which means that they can be applied to all possible movements –blade, quillions, arm, feet, etc–. They are a tool to help us not an end in itself.

THE TARGETS

These are the points in the fencer's chest and head that can be attacked. The targets are chosen depending on the positions of the bodies and blades but, in general, the ones most often aimed for are the right chest and the head.

It is related to the Right Angle as the Planes of Intersection are created by the imaginary extension from the point or edge of the sword to the target in the adversary's body or head.

The targets are used in combination with the Lines to create the planes of intersection.

The planes of intersection are normally formed by the lines of the two swords –the blades– and the blanks in the *diestro's* and his adversary's chest. Simple rules must be applied here.

A The point of the sword should aim to the adversary's chest in long lines –long distances– while in shorter

Figure 1: Lines and planes in the adversary's body.

lines it is acceptable to have it at 45° when performing *atajos*, beats, etc.

B   The intersection plane must be performed with all the blade from its point to the handle and it should start in the Center of Proportion in the third degree of the *diestro's* sword in all cases, either binds virtual and real *atajos* or expulsions.

C   To implement the planes correctly, the *diestro* should not extend the arm into the strict Right Angle position too soon, but instead they should use small Obtuse Angles until they have reached the Proportional Mean. Extending the arm in the Mean of Proportion as shown in the drawings of treatises is nowadays incorrect, as using masks, sneakers and the influence of competitive training makes the way we fence definitely different than in the XVII century. The arm should be extended swiftly and progressively going from blade positions in the Obtuse Angle towards the strict Right Angle position when the Mean is shortened. It is by far more difficult than bluntly using the strict Right Angle position and avoiding taking the complex decision of when and how extending the arm and with which angle and speed, but fencing correctly is not easy. Great fencers always extend the arm at the right moment within the right distance and with the correct speed and rhythm. To achieve this, thousands of hours in the plastron are needed and it has to be like that.

THE LINE

The lines are used to describe either the imaginary way of the blade –that may be circular or straight– or the imaginary ways for the feet, arms, and body.

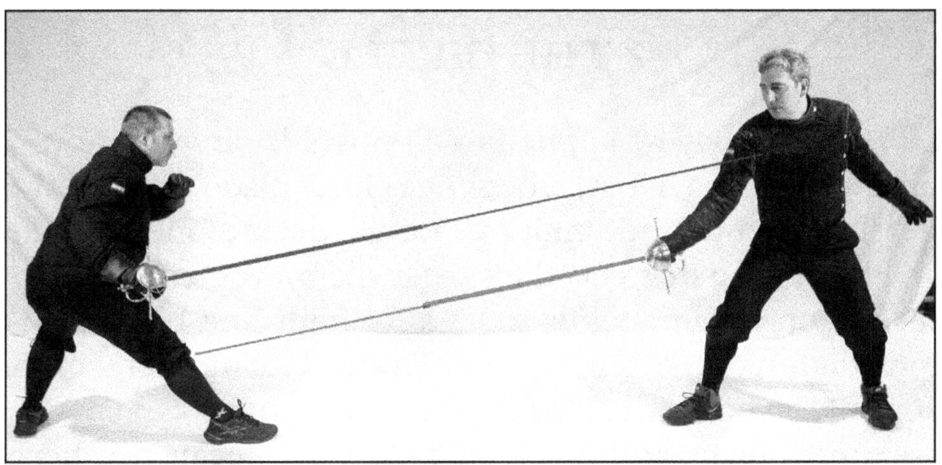

Figure 2: Swords in parallel lines because the lines of the swords do not cross.

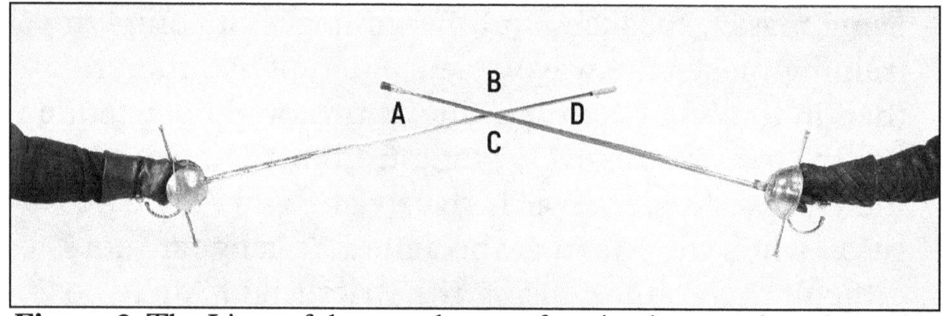

Figure 3: The Lines of the swords cross forming intersection planes (A, B, C, D).

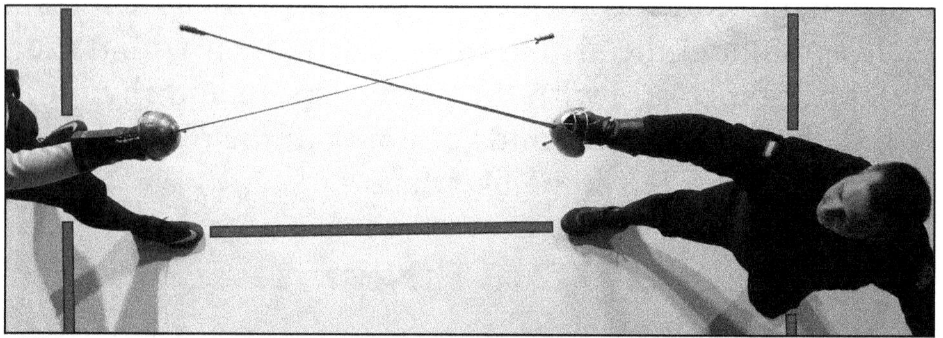

Figure 4: Lines of the swords and feet in the horizontal plane, Infinite Lines are also shown.

THE CIRCLE

The circle may be applied to all possible circular movements; feet, hips, wrist, elbow, shoulder, blade. It is used to measure circular movement using the degrees in the circle. The higher the degrees, the slower the movement is, for this reason a *diestro* tends to look for body and blade positions that may shorten the circular movement of any of the parts of the body involved in movement, so he can spend less time moving and thusly be faster, not because of his speed but because he uses shorter movements.

This is also the reason why, normally, a *diestro* will not circle around the opponent, as walking in the perimeter of a circle is always slower than simply turning in the center of it, and so other forms of movement are more frequently used.

CIRCLES ON THE GROUND

The great circle

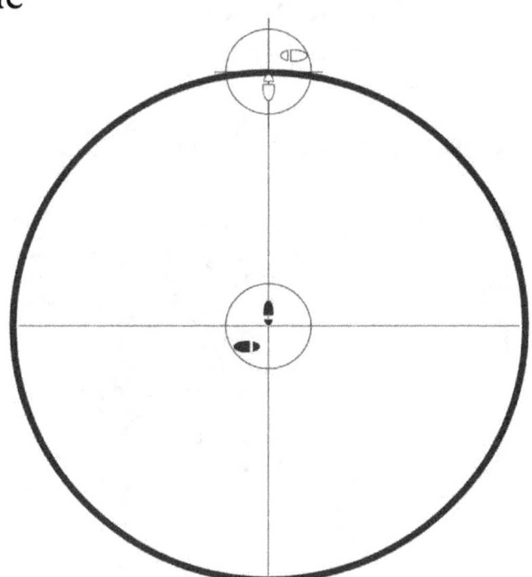

Figure 5: The great circle.

The common circle

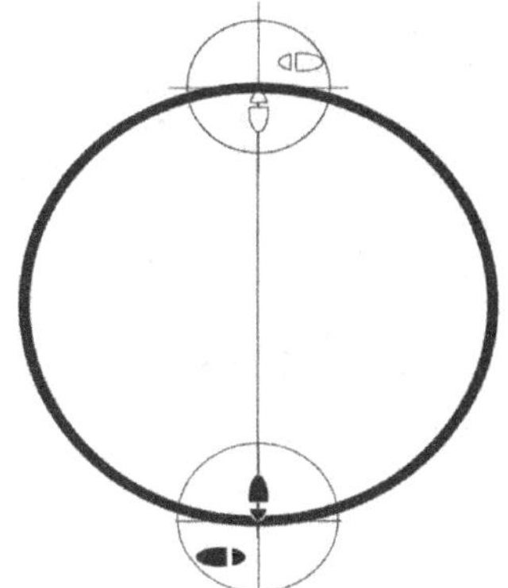

Figure 6: The common circle

The small circle

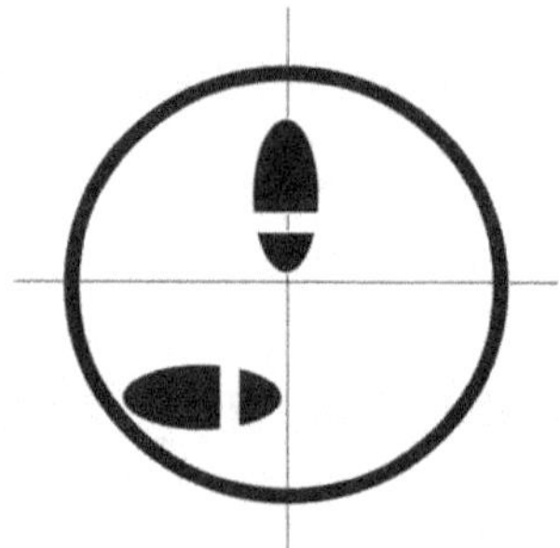

Figure 7: The small circle

CIRCLES ON THE CHEST

Figure 8: The circles in the adversary's chest.

They are used to describe the circular movement of the blade either with the point or with the edge; as I already explained, the greater the circle the slower the movement would be.

A. Quarter circle.
B. 39% Circle Small Portion.
C. Half circle.
D. 70% Circle Large Portion.
E. Full Circle.

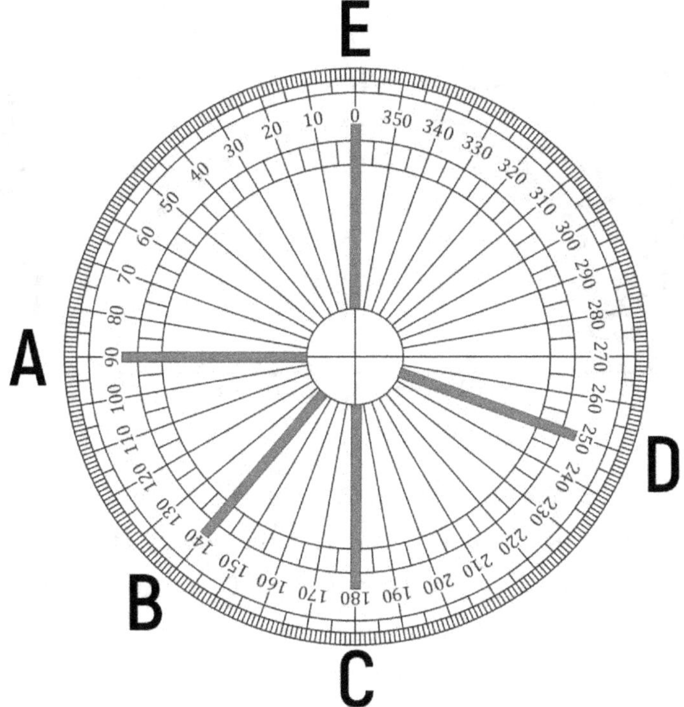

Figure 9: Circle degrees.

THE TRIANGLE

Triangles are geometrical figures often used to measure and analyze the position of the chest compared to the sword and are very useful to explain which targets are open and therefore in danger and which are covered and safe behind the sword.

Destreza normally uses the three geometrical types –scalene, isosceles and equilateral– but the type of triangle is irrelevant in terms of the Practice, the important thing is to understand where it is when it has to be open and when it has to be closed.

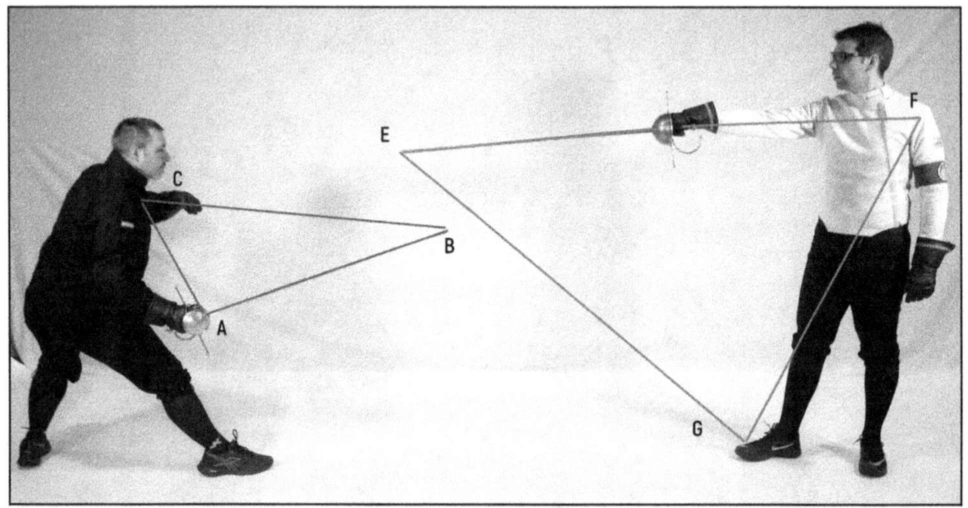

Figure 10: Triangles.

In the picture above, the triangle **ABC** is also the **open** angle; we will talk about it later. The vertical triangle **EFG** is now **closed**. And there is another triangle under the arm of the fencer.

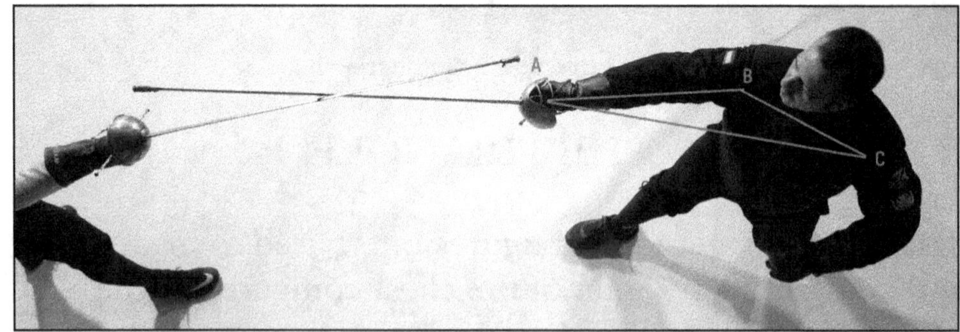

Figure 11: The triangle from a cenital perspective

THE SQUARE

Usually, this figure is only used inscribed inside the circle and it is called the quadrangle, but it is not normally used. Thibault payed attention to it but mostly to try to create a different geometrical method, probably to avoid admitting he was a follower of Spanish *Destreza*. I personally prefer to base the theory in the circle and not the square as it is pretty useless to explain movement; the basic figures in the Spanish tradition are the circle and the triangle.

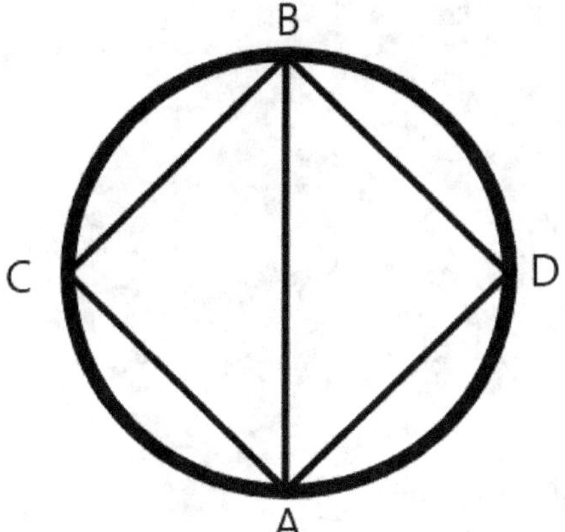

Figure 12: Circle and quadrangle.

Here the quadrangle is used in the context of the great circle, but normally it is more useful when using the Common Circle.

On the chest, the figure of the Parallelogram is used to describe the area between the two collateral lines and the lines in the chest –*Contingencia*– and waist –*Horizontal*–.

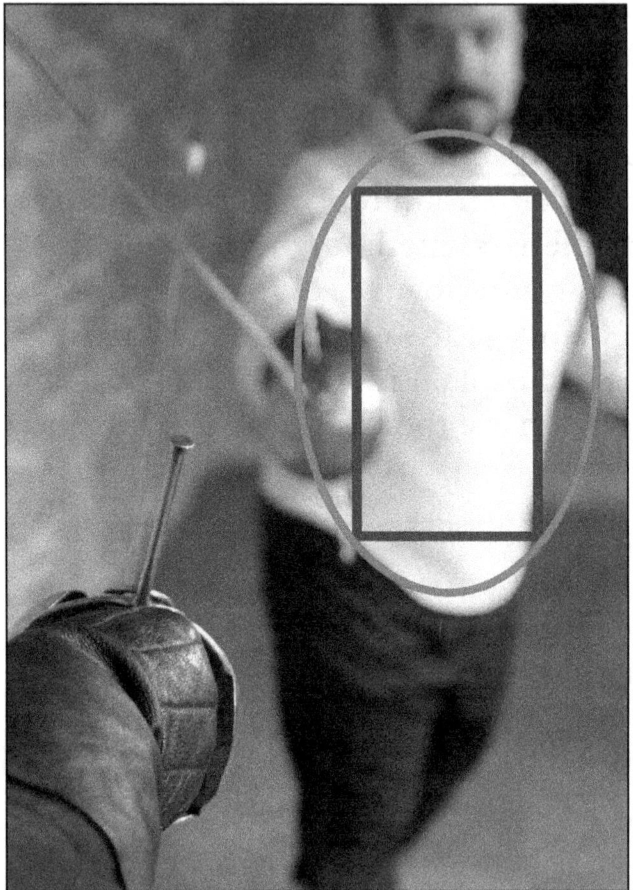

Figure 13: Circle and quadrangle in human's chest.

3 RELATIVE POSITIONS BETWEEN THE DIESTROS

THE DIAMETER

It's the line that bind both fencers when they are in the common circle. There are three diameters:

- The ground diameter. Colored **red** in the picture below.
- The waist diameter. Colored **orange** in the picture below.
- The shoulder diameter. Colored **blue** in the picture below.

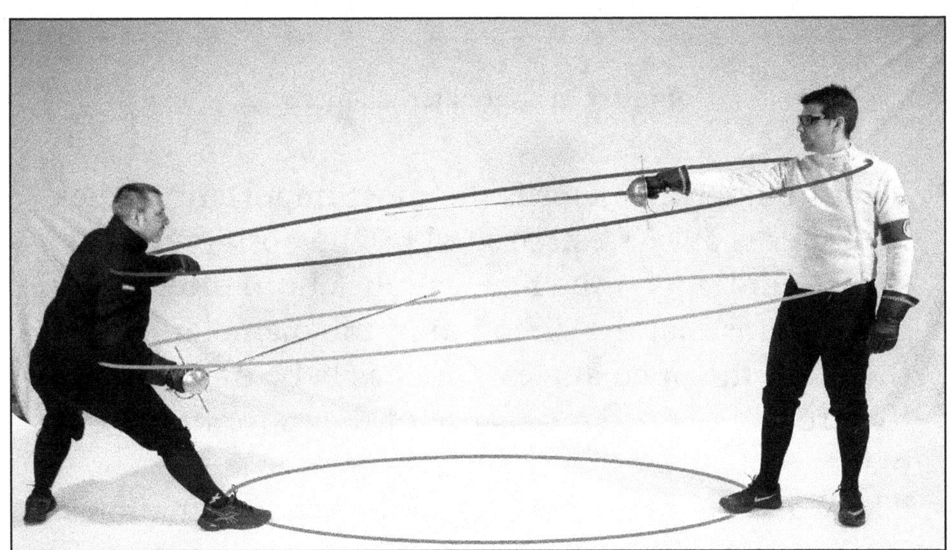

Figure 14: The diameters.

The most important ones are the ground diameter and the shoulder diameter; mostly the last one, as most fencing actions take place at shoulder level. It is also called Central Line or Center.

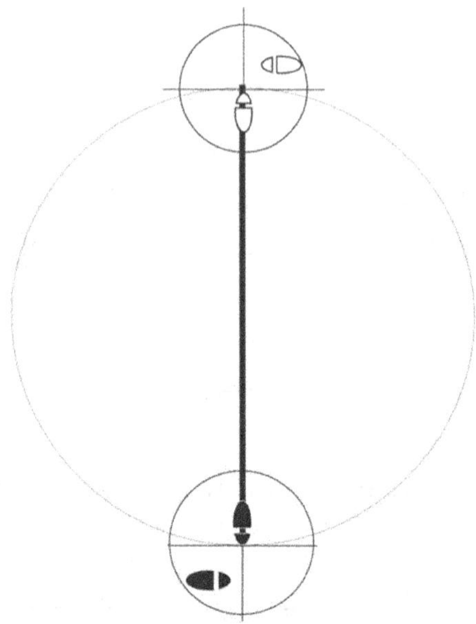

Figure 15: Shoulder Diameter.

A. The shoulder diameter is the most important as the diameter is always established by the position of the swords and not by the feet, as it has been often believed. This means that the direction of the diameter –and therefore the open angles– can easily be different from the ground diameter, because of the movement of the blades.

B. The Waist diameter is rarely needed in explanations, but it is useful to know that exists. The Waist is one of the tools the *diestro* has to change the distance and the angles swiftly, while keeping balance.

C. The Ground Diameter is the diameter we always find drawn in treatises. This diameter is considered to be in the inferior plane and it is achieved through footwork.

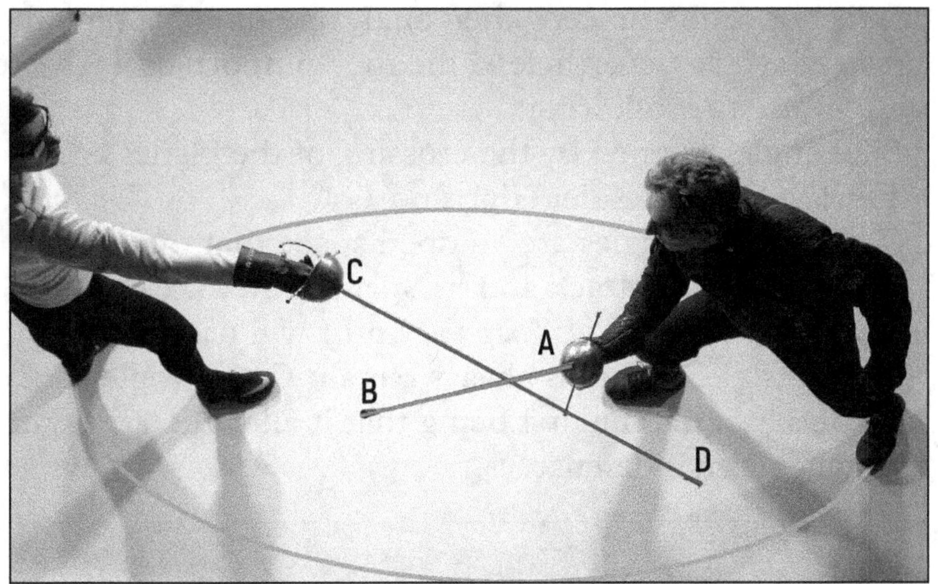

Figure 16: Shoulder Diameter.

The last image shows the shoulder diameter **AB** is the diameter of the diestro in black while **CD** is the diameter of the diestro in white.

In *Destreza* terms, the black has achieved a particular diameter, therefore gaining control of the central line.

As we can see, the ground diameter of the white *diestro* is not the same as the shoulder diameter.

THE ANGLES

One of the most useful concepts in *Destreza* are the Angles. There are many places from where angles may be measured; for example, the angle of the body and the main arm, the angle formed by the arm and the sword, the angles formed by the arm and the chest of the *diestro*, the angle formed by the position of the feet etc. Their use is up to the teacher or the fencer, when analyzing or explaining the phrase of arms. Nevertheless, the most important angles to consider are the following:

I. The angles formed by the crossing of the blades are four: Inside, Outside, High and Low.

    Two of these angles are an open space that the adversary can use to attack and in Spanish they are called *Angulo de Capacidad Ocupable* and I will use the term Open Angle. There is always a main Open Angle and a secondary one, the first being that it allows a larger gap in the enemy's defense.

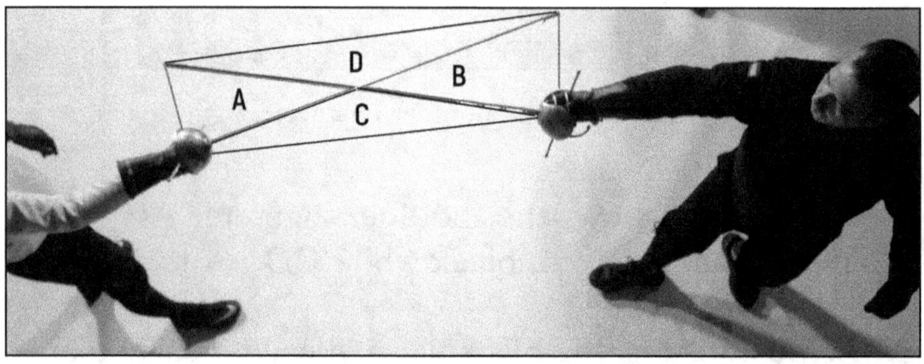

Figure 17: The open angles.

The important Angle to consider here for the *diestro* in black are **B** –his own inside line– **D** –his own outside line– and **C** –the Open Angle from where he can reach his opponent–.

II. The vertical angle formed by the body and the arm, represented as **A** and **B** in the following picture.

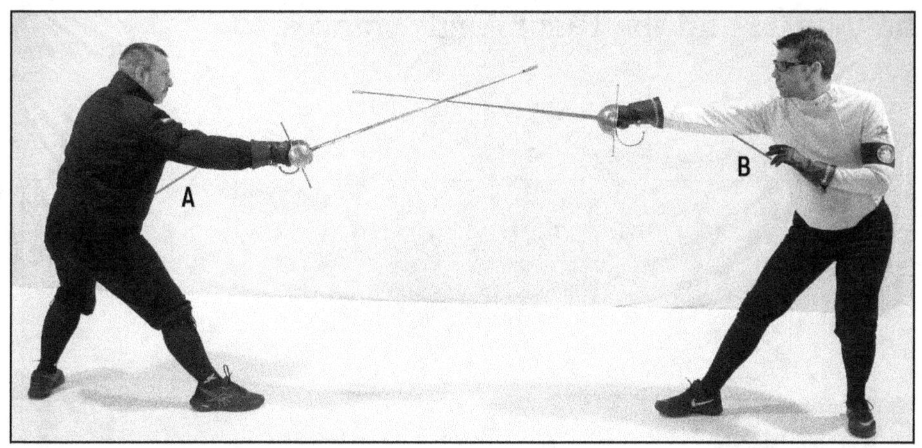

Figure 18: The vertical angle.

III. The Right, Acute and Obtuse Angle are the three angles to be considered.

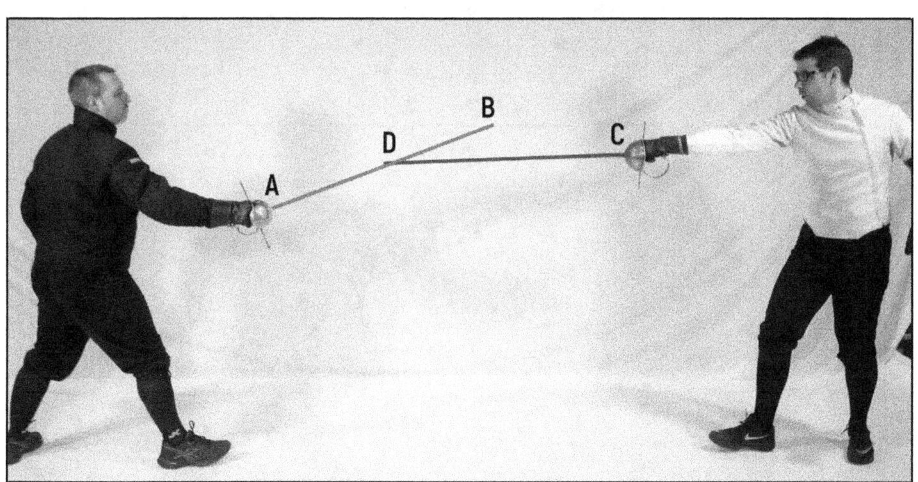

Figure 19: Diestro in black standing in obtuse angle. Diestro in white standing in right angle.

The Obtuse and the Right Angle stances.

The Obtuse Angle.

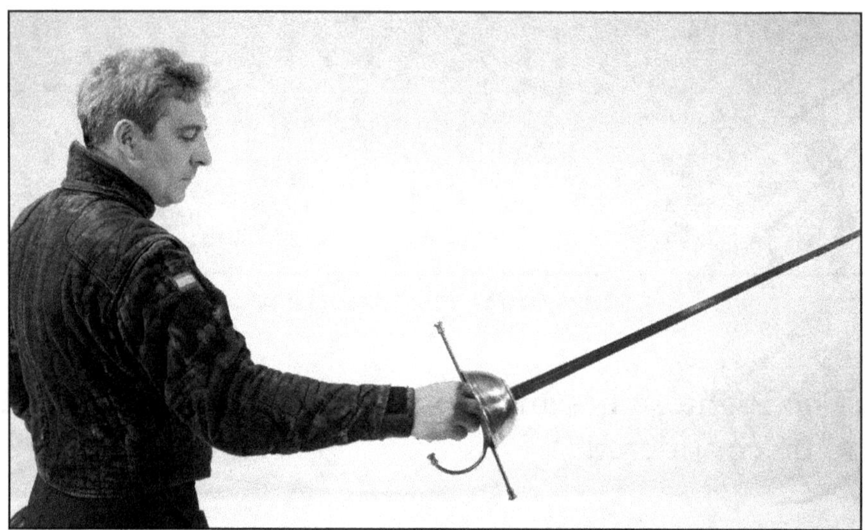

Figure 20: Diestro standing in obtuse angle.

The Acute angle.

Figure 21: Diestro standing in acute angle.

IV. The horizontal angle formed by the chest of the *diestro* and the sword arm. The triangles are formed from this angle.

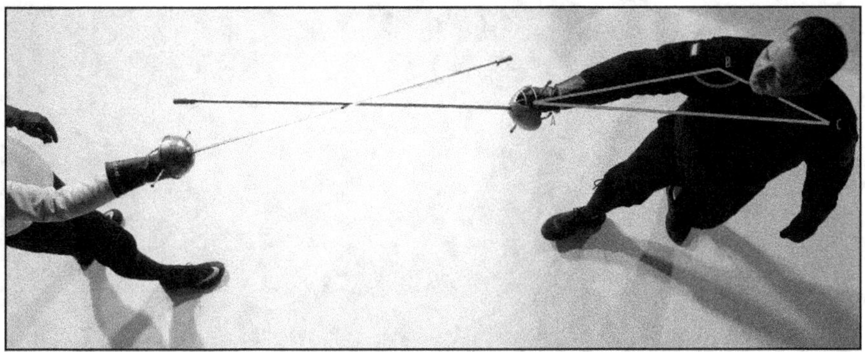

Figure 22: Horizontal angle.

V. The angle formed on the ground plane by the positions of the feet (90° or 45°, as an example).

Figure 23: Angles on the ground plane.

VI. The angle formed by the sword and the arm. This is usually called Mixed Angle when the sword and the arm are not in a straight line.

Figure 24: Mixed angle defined in the black diestro's arm and blade.

THE MOVEMENTS OF THE BLADE

Destreza has terms to describe the direction of the blade movement; these movements are meant to offer the fencer descriptive terms that allow simple and exact fencing explanations.

These movements are:

- *Violento:* Upward movement of the sword – Ascending cut.
- *Natural:* Downward movement – Descending cut.
- *Accidental:* Onward movement of the sword – Thrust.
- *Extraño:* Backward movement.
- *Remiso:* Lateral movement from center to one side.

- *De Reducción:* Returning movement form one side to the center.

Blade movements are not always meant to attack. Most of the time they are used to describe preparation actions as binding, *atajo*, deflections, etc. Additionally, very often these movements are very small, and performed at high speed, using all the possible angles, obtuse, right and acute depending on the situation.

The movements can be combined among them, the most common mixes movements are the mixed movement of *natural*, *de reducción* and *accidental* when thrusting directly from a cut or *extraño*, *violento* and *remiso* when performing ceding parries.

4. ACTIONS IN THE INFERIOR PLANE

THE FOOTWORK

Destreza footwork is not different from other types of footwork in practical terms though theoretically it is more detailed as the direction of the steps are named in order to be understood and used when techniques are performed.

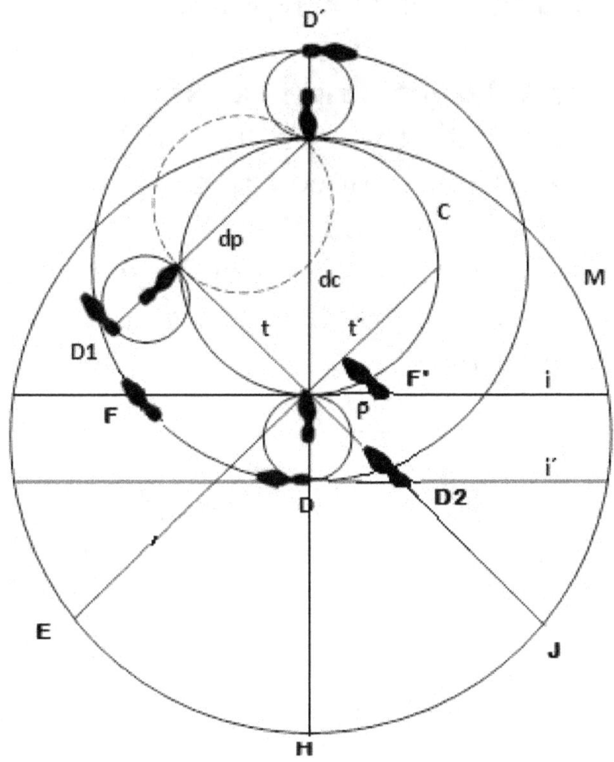

The basic steps are:

- Forward step: **dc**
- Backward step: **PD** Right foot **DH** left foot

- Diagonal step forward: Right and left **t** and **t'**
- Lateral step: Right and left **I** and **I'**
- Curve step: Right foot **PF'** Left foot **DF** and **DF"**

These steps are normally combined in order to handle distance in a more efficient way; they are not performed rigidly and statically but swiftly, in a fluid and subtle way. Those who walk with a constant slow rhythm may be using the described steps but they are using them in a non-efficient way, and they will always be easily defeate.

Special combinations of steps are:

1. **Mixed step lateral and rear step.** The one used to step back, usually towards the left or right side. **DE** or **PJ** If we are right-handed the more important one is the one to the left side, and *Destreza* treatises normally refer only to this one. I have included also the one to the right side because practical experience proves it can be used sometimes.

Figure 25: Diestro in black performing a mixed step lateral and rear step.

2. Mixed Step of diagonal and curve step. The one used for the *movimiento de conclusión.*

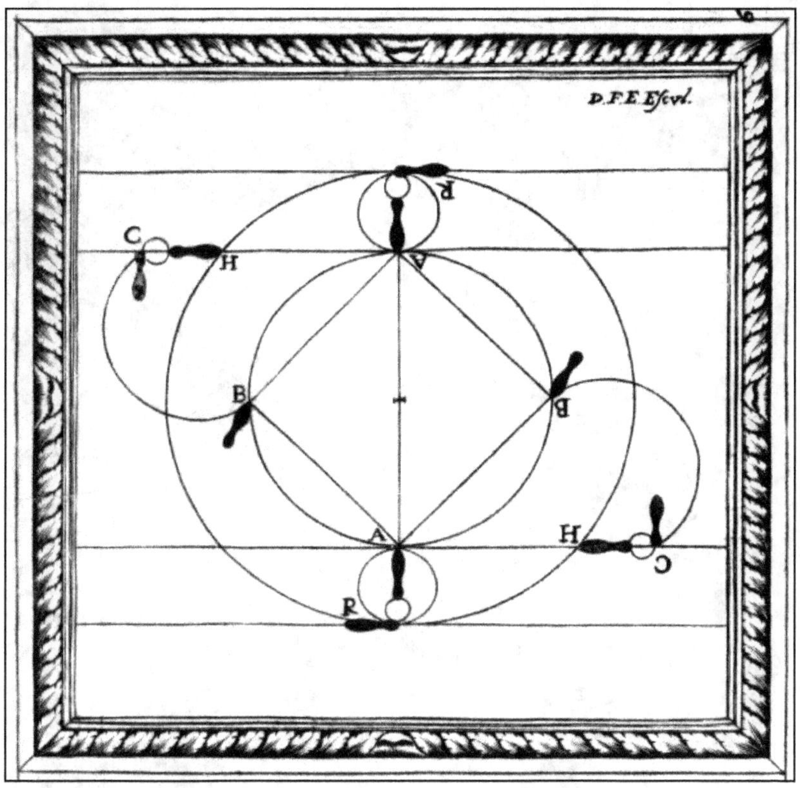

Figure 26: Mixed Step of diagonal and curve.

The right foot is represented with the **ABC** positions, while the left foot is represented with the **RH** positions. The diagonal step is performed using the right foot while the curved step is done with the left one. At the end of the movement the *diestro* ends with the left foot leading.

Figure 27: Diestro in black performing a mixed Step of diagonal and curve.

The illustration is theoretical; in practical terms, the technique must be performed while bending the knees and leaning the body forwards and backwards to perform it in a mechanically efficient way. If done while standing, it will not work –on the contrary–, most probably the adversary will turn, and it will be them the ones making the *Movimiento de Conclusión*.

Train your legs and body, bend your knees and use strong, stable positions from where you can move fast.

5. STANCES AND MEANS

THE STANCES

Destreza focuses on movement, which means that to properly apply the theory and perform techniques correctly movement must be carefully trained. Here I include the basic stances the human body can use in Fencing; I suggest not to consider them as static positions but to consider that they are used in swift movement, so the *diestro* will have to change them constantly, sometimes performing them shorter, sometimes longer, higher or lower depending on what is necessary. The stances, just like everything else in *Destreza*, are a tool, not an end in themselves.

The *diestro*, if he really is a *diestro*, will adapt to the circumstances in order to hit without being hit. I have included stances coming from other traditions like the *botta dritta* of the Napolitan School and *el quiebro* of the vulgar, as they can be used in certain circumstances very effectively.

A. *Bella Española* stance.

Similar to the *guardia di terza* stance of many Italian authors, it is the Stance used when the diestro is in out of reach distance.

We do not place the hand on the chest to avoid losing the correct profile of the body. When necessary, though, the left hand may be brought forward; but only when it is necessary.

This Stance may be performed with 2, 2.5 or 3 feet length depending on the fencer and the context.

Figure 28: Bella Española stance.

B. The standing stance.

This stance is mainly used when the *diestro* wants to move sideways, as the *Bella Española* stance does not allow for a fluid lateral movement. For this reason, the *diestro* normally raises to place themselves in a more comfortable position to move to any of their sides. The blade is shown here in the Right Angle position, but it could also be used in obtuse or acute position. There is not one single standing position as there is not one single *Bella Española* stance; a lot of different variations exist: it is up to the *diestro* to choose among them, we must not forget that Fencing is an Art, the Science must be brought into a concrete practical form by the *diestro*; there is no escaping from this fact.

Figure 29: Standing stance.

C. The lunge or body forward stance – *Extremo de cuerpo adelante*.

The lunge, or rather, the extension of the body leaning forward to reduce distance, is one of the ways the *diestro* has to not only to hit, but also to get closer and thus changing from a Mean to another.

The lunge should never be overextended, especially if it is used in combination with a preparatory action.

When using this stance, the *diestro* should not forget to have both feet well placed on the ground and to shift the body weight with the waist, relying on the strength of the legs and the bending of the knees for the waist movement.

Figure 30: Diestro in black performing a lunge. *Extremo de cuerpo Adelante.*

D. The body backward stance –*Extremo de cuerpo atrás* or *Quiebro*–.

The body backwards stance is not often described as a *Destreza* Stance but rather as one of the vulgar techniques known as *el Quiebro*. It is also pictured by Francesco Alfieri in his treatise and with a slight interesting variation by Pallavicini. I include it here because the stance may be efficiently used if performed to control the Means and not as a technique. The hand position must be nails-under; if it is performed nails-out the true edge would be badly placed for any kind of control or preparatory actions. Additionally, from the symmetry point of view, it is the opposite of the Body Forward Stance, but it must not be used as the basic stance; this position must be used wisely and in the right moment.

From this position, the adversary's blade can be controlled from the outside line but not from the inside line which means that if it is used against inside line attacks

–I do not suggest, it as a rule–, the sword is useless for defense and probably the left hand should be used for that purpose.

As I've said before, I prefer to use this stance against attacks on the outside line.

Figure 31: The body backwards stance. *Extremo de cuerpo Atrás.*

E. The italian stance, known in italy as *Botta dritta.*

The Italian stance was described by Marcelli and Pallavicini and taught in Spain by Pérez de Mendoza and Ettenhard and, probably, it was also used by Rejón da Silva.

Though it is not part of the traditional Destreza theory I include it here again as a part of the necessary movement to travel from any rear stance to the forward one. This stance is achieved by extending the front leg but without displacing the weight of the body forward, unlike in the Lunge. The forwarded leg is not bent but the weight of the body is slightly kept between both legs. This stance teaches the diestro how to properly handle weight displacement when changing stance. I do not recommend using it as an executive preconceived thrust unless the mechanics of this stance are completely mastered.

Figure 32: The Italian stance.

F. The passing step.

The passing step is one of the most important steps to make fluid and effective movements in fencing, which is one of the basic principles in *Destreza*. There is no way to move swiftly if the passing step is not used; double single steps and passing steps must be combined to make movement efficient and safe.

The passing step may be used either in preparatory actions or in executive ones, those meant to hit. The advantage of this step is that it allows to make a number of movements with the sword hand with only one step, which is easier on a coordination level than performing three movements with the hand in two different steps, something that is more difficult by far.

The passing step must be performed without losing balance. For this reason, is necessary to avoid having the feet too close to one another; if this happens, the position will be very unstable; if the feet are too far apart, the stance will lack depth: it will work well in preparatory actions but it will not be useful to hit. The passing step is normally performed stepping somewhat to the left, no matter if the action is performed on the inside or on the outside line.

In the following picture, the passing step is shown when performing a thrust in *Ángulo Mixto*, an action known in the vulgar Practice as *Enarcada*.

Figure 33: Diestro in black performing passing step.

THE MEANS OF MEASUREMENTS

I am not a native English speaker and I am not completely sure of many things I write in English, nevertheless, this translation loses the aristotelic meaning of Mean as a vehicle to achieve something and concentrates exclusively on the spatial meaning, that is why I will use the term Mean. If it is incorrect, please let me know.

The Means are the concept *Destreza* uses to measure movement which is the base of every fencing action. Movement implies Time and Space but it cannot be measured from the Time perspective, so *Destreza* focuses on the Space point of view. Once Distance can be measured and Time scatters from Distance, in terms of measuring.

To measure something, we need parameters and to that end we use the elements we have seen before.

IIt is very important to pay attention to the fact that all Means must be considered and calculated from the quillions of the *diestro's* sword, as expressed in all *Destreza* treatises. How the *diestro* gets there is up to him; the important thing is to put the sword in the right place and position.

To put it shortly, all calculations must be done from the sword, not the feet, because the Diameter the *diestro* needs to study is the one where swordplay takes place not the one on the ground. Do not forget this, or quite often geometrical calculations will not work.

The Means are an angle and a distance in a set moment, so they must be learned through practice and experience; the better we learn how to measure them and use them, the better fencers we will be.

Please consider that nowadays to get them and use them properly the arm cannot be extended in Mean of Proportion as treatises suggest: they did not use masks and sneakers and doing this made sense back then but now it does not. By doing so in our modern-day context we will expose ourselves unnecessarily and go against the most basic *Destreza* principle of controlling the Central Line, thus losing. And if we cannot perform *Destreza* in an effective way we are not doing any good to the Spanish tradition. This is a different time and we are different people, only by fencing correctly will we honorably defend *Destreza's* place in modern day fencing.

The Means must be achieved through footwork and overall movement, so they basically need training and learning how and when to properly extend the arm.

A. Out of range.

The fencers are at a distance where, if they extended the arms, the points of their swords would not reach the quillions of the adversary's sword. Out of Range includes a large variety of distances; some may be closer to Mean of Proportion some may be further away from it, some may be performed in lower stances and others in higher stances, but all of them are almost always done with the sword in obtuse angle.

The assault normally starts here, so it is necessary to learn how to get closer without being hit. No parameter is established here, that is why I do not consider it a Mean but a simple Distance. This concept was not described in *Destreza's* traditional theory, but we include it as nowadays we are forced to start fencing here and use *Atajo virtual* before getting into the Mean of Proportion. In my opinion there is no point in denying this fact, as even those who do not want to use it start fencing Out of Range and often have problems trying to get closer when their opponent is skillful.

When you teach, as I do every day, you need to use the term Out of Range constantly, so I finally decided to include it in the Theory to make it easier for teachers and students.

Figure 34: Out of range Mean.

B. Mean of proportion.

The Mean of Proportion can be defined as a distance and an angle in a set moment.

The fencers are at the distance where if they extend the arms the point of their blades –if the swords have the same length– are at the quillions level. Authors vary on this subject: some use the weak, others the handle, and others the pommel, depending on how they fenced; so we can't know which one is better for us nowadays by following them. I suggest my students to roughly consider that the point of their blade should be near the quillions but that they can adjust it as they prefer as long they are not too far nor too close.

It is necessary to understand that the Mean of Proportion is a theoretical point, not a physical one; usually, in the assault, skilled fencers go directly from Out of Range to shorter means as the Proportional Mean or the Proportionate Mean. It is not necessary to step on the Mean of Proportion –on the contrary–, this may often be dangerous and useless.

From the Mean of Proportion the *diestro* cannot hit his adversary in a single movement, not even with a lunge; he will need two steps to get a hit. And remember, you do not need to step in the Mean of Proportion, you are free to use the Means as it suits you better. Train footwork and move as good as you can; the better your movement is, the easier you will get the right means in every case.

Also, it is not necessary to go into the Mean of Proportion while standing, it can also be done lunging, dodging or advancing sideways etc. the important thing is to know the distance and know how to handle it. It is also not necessary to always extend the arm in the Right Angle. The figure is only meant to measure the distance but it is not a technique, the arm can stay obtuse and the suddenly get into the Right Angle position for a powerful thrust. This is perfectly correct if coverage is good and the central line stays controlled.

I include here three different body positions and angles that show how the Mean of Proportion can be attained and played from a lot of different positions, not only standing.

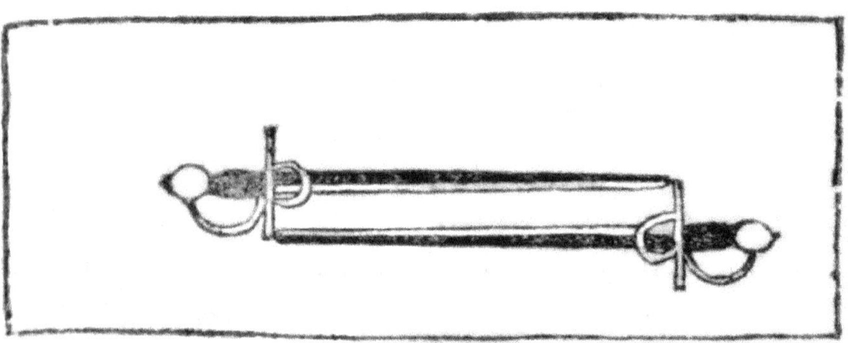

Figure 35: Mean of Proportion in Luis Pacheco de Narváez's *Grandezas de la espada*.

Figure 36: Mean of Proportion with Atajo in the beginning with Right Angle stance (Diestro on the left) against Obtuse Angle stance (Diestro on the right).

Figure 37: Mean of Proportion with both swords in Obtuse angle with Diestro on the left performing Atajo in the inside traveling to the Proportional Mean.

Figure 38: Mean of Proportion with Obtuse (Diestro on the left) against Acute Angle stance (Diestro on the right).

C. Proportional mean.

This Mean was not described by Pacheco, he disregarded the theoretical description of it, though he unavoidably used it it as it can be seen in his diagrams. It was later described by Lorenz de Rada, to have a more complete picture when handling space.

Figure 39: Proportional Mean with Atajo in the outside achieved by Diestro on the left.

This mean is halfway between the mean of proportion and proportionate mean and it is normally achieved by stepping with the left foot towards either side or with the right foot to the right side. From MP, a curve step will bring us to MPL but it is often reached, on the left side, by changing the position of the legs and the feet during the movement. In the right side it can only be performed with curve steps towards that side.

Often, the Proportional Mean is achieved only by the movement of the shoulders, hips, and small steps if there is blade contact. Large steps are normally not used if there is not blade contact, but may be very useful if the *diestro* has controlled the Central Line.

From the proportional mean the *diestro* can touch the adversary with the extension of the arm and step.

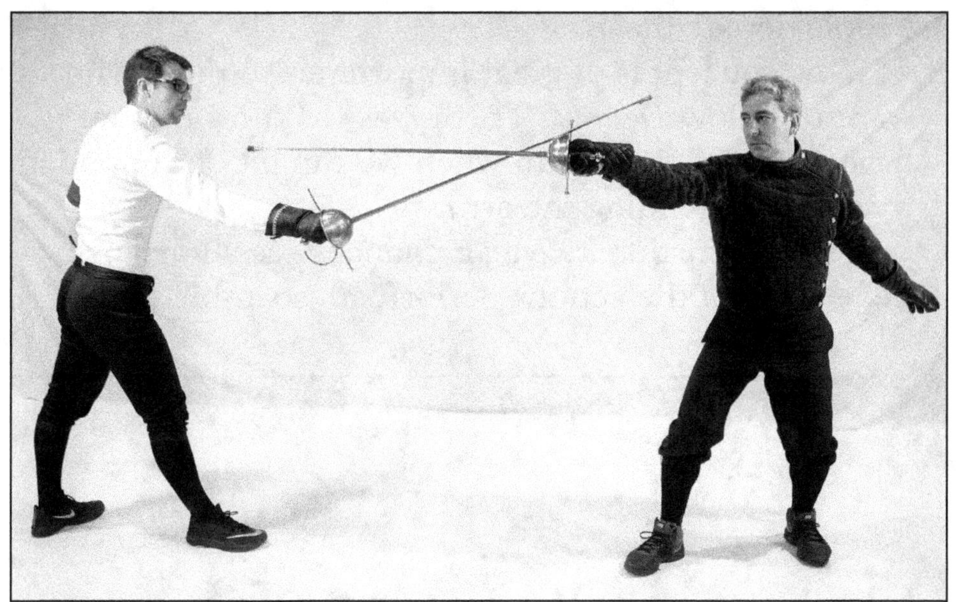

Figure 40: Proportional Mean with Atajo in the Inside using a curve step towards the left side by Diestro in black.

This image shows the position of the feet in the Proportional Mean which is defined by the curve line **DF** for the left foot and **PF'** for the right foot. The position shown above it is a perfect example of the use of this line. It will also be possible to move the right foot to the right side using the line **D – D2**, turning the body towards the right side.

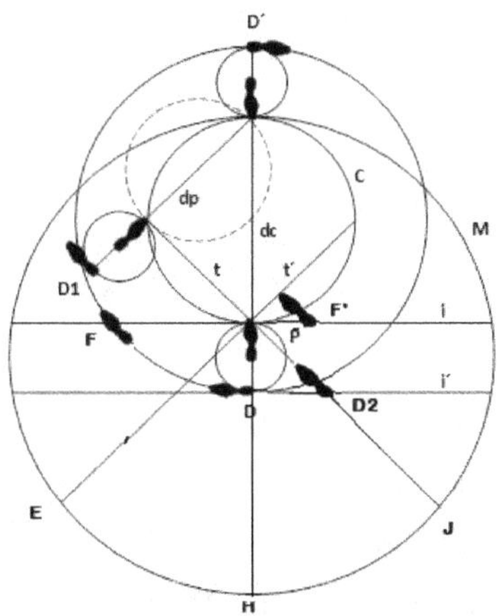

D. Proportionate mean.

This concept is of great importance to those who want to follow *Destreza* Theory, as we know that we have achieved this Mean when we can hit our opponent by simply extending the arm.

The Proportionate Mean changes –as all means do–, depending of the actions performed, so a thrust will

Figure 41: Proportionate Mean with thrust delivered by Atajo in the inside and a transversal passing step in the Right Collateral Line by Diestro in black.

have a different Proportionate Mean than a cut or a disarm.

Besides the sword length, the Proportionate Mean also changes depending on the place where the action is performed, because of the aspects –shoulder alignment–, and because of the position of the legs and feet, as all these factors may make the Proportionate Mean to be closer or further.

It is necessary to pay attention to the fact that the diameter must be consider and defined by the blade position which means that all Means may be achieved moving in a straight or almost straight line when the point of the adversary's sword leaves the central line and leaves an opening. When this happens, we have a particular diameter and we must enter the open gap either with the

Figure 42: Proportionate Mean with Atajo on the Outside performed with Body Forward Stance by Diestro on the left.

Figure 43: Proportionate Mean with thrust on the Inside with long passing step in the Right Collateral Line by Diestro in black.

Figure 44: Proportionate Mean with Tajo in the inside and a Left Transversal step by Diestro in black.

Figure 45: Proportionate Mean with Angulo Mixto in the Outside with Body Forward Stance by Diestro in the left.

Figure 46: Proportionate Mean of the Movimiento de Conclusión before the end of the technique. Here is performed with Atajo in the Inside and Right High Line by Diestro in the left.

sword or with the body. What I mean is that stepping sideways in long lines is not correct, on the contrary, is a big mistake that our adversary can easily turn to their advantage; sideway steps must be used only when the adversary's blade is under control –with any kind of blade contact– or it is so far from the diameter that it cannot possibly reach the *diestro*.

In this last case there is no lunge because if there was the blade would go through the strong of the enemy's blade, so a higher stance is a better option. *Ángulo mixto* is the *Destreza* version of *enarcada*.

To end this first part please consider that this text is not exhaustive in any way, many things have been left out for time reasons.

The small amount of Practical Theory shown here, is what I have learned and taught throughout the years; through it I do not pretend to reconstruct any style nor any particular author, I have studied all of them but I am open to learn from any style, method, teacher, re-searcher as long as what they do convinces me; my aim is to fence properly and, above all, to teach people to fence correctly.

ABOUT THE AUTHOR

Alberto Bomprezzi started his martial artist career practicing karate in the Shotokan school in the early eighties, eventually switching to sport fencing, where he competed at national level until 2001, the year he retired to start researching and teaching historical fencing.

In 2002 he founded the AEEA (Asociación Española de Esgrima Antigua) with only the Madrid group, but in a few years the number grew and now schools all over Spain work to spread historical fencing in the Spanish territory. Since 2006, he is a professional fencing teacher, the only one in Spain who is strictly focused on historical fencing.

His main interest is body mechanics as a way to develop practical methods that may be applied to all kind of straight double-edged weapons through training. To that extent he trains and teaches longsword, sword and buckler, montante, cut and thrust, all kind of rapiers alone and with dagger and/or buckler.

From the theoretical and historical point of view, he studies all sources that may be useful to learn and improve, mainly from Italian and German origin. He mainly uses, researches and teaches *La Verdadera Destreza*, the Spanish theoretical method of the XVI and XVII century based on geometry which he uses as a tool to analyze fencing and develop a true practical method for the use of historical weapons. He also has an interest in the southern XVII century and early XVIII century Italian style because of its close relationship with the Spanish method.

In academical terms he teaches historical fencing to students of History in the Universidad Complutense de Madrid. He was invited to participate in the 1st Congress of Military History held in 2014 where he gave the lecture *"The military mindset as generator of a theoretical method to be used to learn how to safely face duels"*.

The conference was published in the papers of the congress by Universidad Complutense de Madrid.

He has published articles in the specialized magazines:

- *Arma Blanca* – a specialized magazine on edged weapons
- *Despertaferro* – One of the most important History magazines in Spain, for which he often collaborates as an advisor for weapons and fighting styles of the XV, XVI and XVII centuries.

He has also participated in history documentaries on TV since 2004:

- 2004 *El Madrid de Alatriste* made by National Geographic on the XVII century swordsmanship.
- 2015 *El siglo de Águila Roja* made by RTVE –Radiotelevisión Española the Spanish National Broadcasting Company– on duels and history of swordsmanship and fencing.

He also he is a permanent teacher for the armament course of the IHCM –the Spanish Institute of Culture and Military History– and collaborates with the Army Museum in Toledo and with the Royal Guard of Spain.

In 2012 he was awarded the Great Cross of the Order of Santa María de España for his work of research and resurrection of *la Verdadera Destreza*.

In 2019 he took part in the Minsk European Games, as a national coach for Portugal and Spain.

In 2019 he participated in the 2nd International Congress *"Ciudad del Compromiso"* in Caspe (Zaragoza) organized by the City Council of Caspe and the University of Zaragoza.